AmericanGirl Libr

More Games and Giggles

Wild About Animals!

SCHOLASTIC INC.
New York Toronto London Auckland Sydney
Mexico City New Delhi Hong Kong Buenos Aires

ISBN 0-439-39061-3

Published by Scholastic Inc., 557 Broadway, New York, NY 10012,
by arrangement with Pleasant Company Publications.

12 11 10 9 8 7 6 5 4 3 4 5 6 7/0

Printed in the U.S.A. 23

First Scholastic printing, February 2002

Editors: Trula Magruder, Michelle Watkins
Designer: Chris Lorette David
Cover Art Direction: Kym Abrams
Cover Design: Marilyn Dawson, Kate Evans

Contents

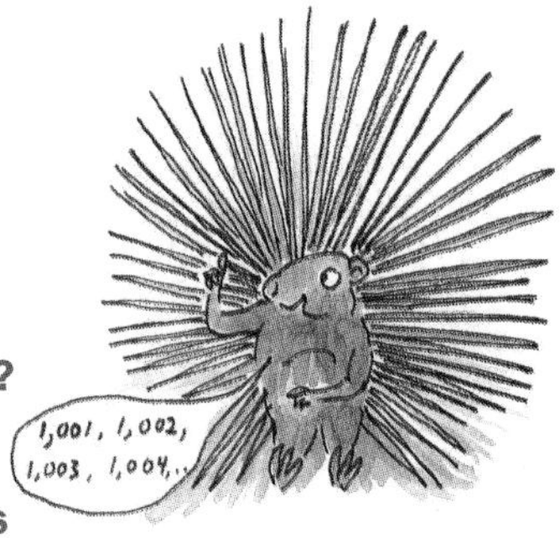

Group Games

Indoor

Outdoor

Picture Puzzles

Crosswords

Brain Benders

Music and Talking Games

Other Great Games

Purr-fect Pet Show

The Giggle Gang's *Purr*-fect Pet Show has turned into a hairy mess! Study the picture for as long as you like. Then turn the page to see how many questions you can answer—without looking back!

Purr-fect Pet Show

How much do you remember about the picture from page 5? Answer the questions and find out.

1. How many dogs is the girl with pigtails walking?
2. Name the three colors of birds in the cage.
3. What is a girl offering to one of the rabbits?
4. Name the two pets a girl is holding in her arms.
5. What is at the bottom of the goldfish bowl?
6. What is the goat standing on?
7. What is the girl doing to the cow?
8. What animal is riding the horse?

Mr. E. Mutt: Owl Ouch

Owlivia woke up with a sore throat. When Mr. E. dropped by, she asked him, "What happens when an owl has a sore throat?" Use the decoder below to see what Mr. E. said.

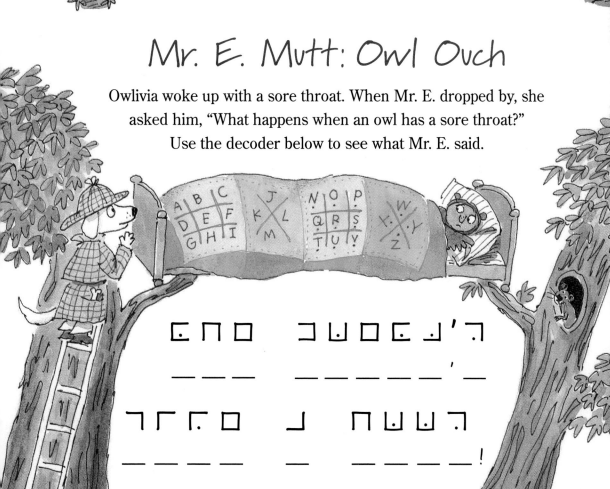

Picture This

Copy the drawing from each box into its matching place in the grid, and you'll create a "Save Me" poster for an endangered animal. The center box is filled in for you.

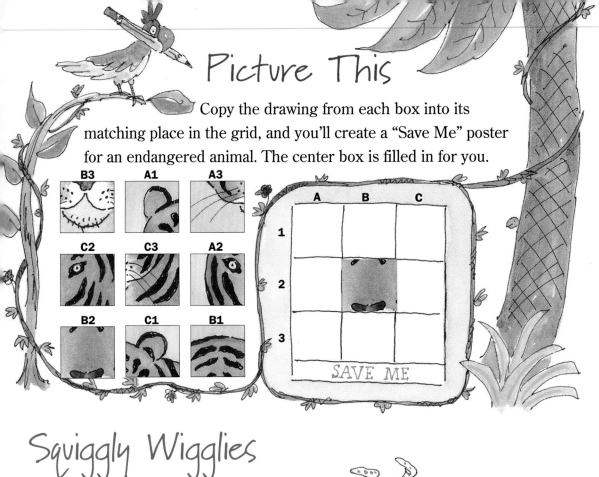

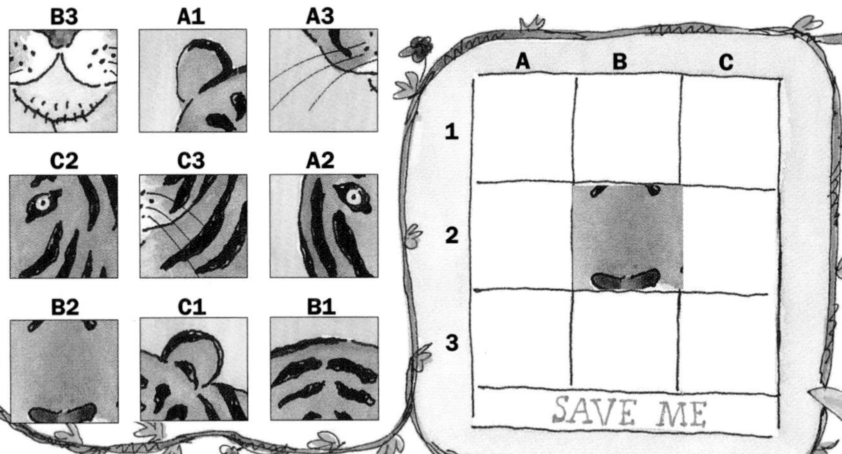

Squiggly Wigglies

No one can resist laughing at the silly animal drawings made from squiggly wigglies! To begin, ask a friend to draw a short, squiggly line on paper. Then you can turn her paper in any direction to create your animal. Now it's her turn. Check out these squiggly wigglies first!

Teacher's Pet

Solve this crossword and move to the head of the class! If you get stuck, check the Word Box for answers.

Our teacher Mrs. Smith and Fluffy by Alexa

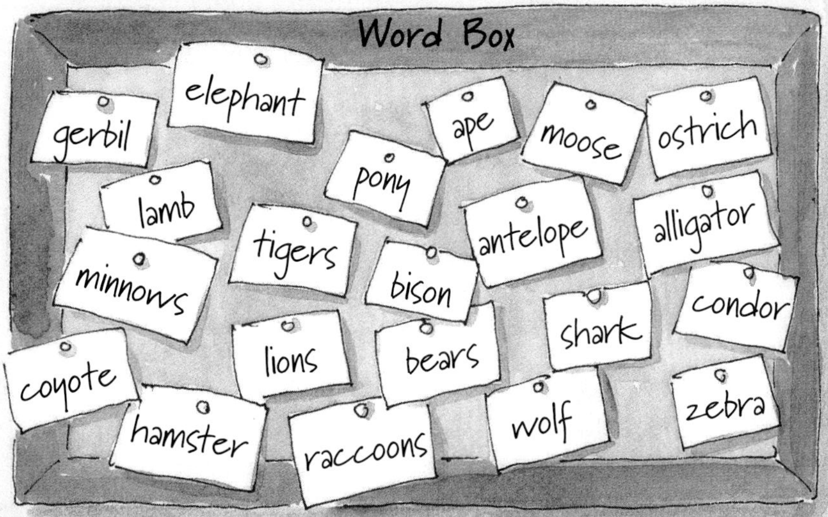

Across

1. Looks like a crocodile but has a blunter snout
4. Mary had a little _______ .
6. The largest kind of deer; sounds like a chocolate dessert
8. These small mammals look like bandits wearing black masks.
10. ". . . where the deer and the _______ play"
12. This wolf relative barks 11 different ways.
15. Small fuzzy pet that sleeps curled in a ball
16. This animal looks like it wears black-and-white-striped pajamas.
17. A small pet with chubby cheeks
18. Term for North American buffalo

Down

2. What Dorothy and the Scarecrow thought might be in the forest: _______ and _______ and _______, oh my!
3. A gorilla
5. Tiny freshwater fish
7. A great white _______
9. It pretended to be Red Riding Hood's grandmother.
11. You can wear your hair in a _______ tail.
12. The world's largest flying bird
13. It can run as fast as a racehorse, and its egg weighs more than 3 pounds.
14. An animal that always travels with its trunk

1.
2.
3.
4.
5.
6.
7.
8.
9.
10.
11.
12.
13.
14.
15.
16.
17.
18.

Bark or Mark

One person barks. One person marks. That's the game!

For this game, you'll need a watch with a second hand or a minute timer, paper, and a pencil. To begin, call out an animal's name. Your opponent has one minute to write words that start with the first letter of the animal's name. To keep her from concentrating, bark, sing, dance—anything except touch her. When her time is up, she calls out an animal and you take a turn. The player with the most words at the end wins. The loser must act like any animal the winner names for one minute. Then go again!

Cross-Outs

What is gray with four legs and a trunk? No, it's not an elephant... Follow the instructions below, then read the answer!

1. Cross out 4 flowers.
2. Cross out 2 games.
3. Cross out 3 school subjects.
4. Cross out 2 insects.
5. Cross out 4 words that mean "happy."

A	Daisy	Ant	Mouse	Science
Tulip	Cheerful	Going	Gym	Elated
Rose	Merry	Art	On	Daffodil
Mosquito	Vacation	Hopscotch	Glad	Checkers

Sea Things

To win season passes to Water World, the Giggle Gang must find at least ten things that start with an "S." See how many you can find, and circle them.

Animal Instincts

Amaze friends with your mental powers by performing this sneaky trick.

Ask one friend to name an animal. Write that animal on a slip of paper, then fold the paper twice. Ask her to name five other animals. Write on five more slips and fold them in the same way. Mix up the slips in a bowl.

To perform your magic, ask another friend to pick a slip of paper from the bowl, open it, and concentrate on the animal she sees. After a bit of "focusing," say the name of the animal she picked.

How do you do it? You write the name of the first animal on all the slips! Don't let anyone see what you write.

Two of a Kind

Circle the set of baby twins in each row below.

1. 

2. 

3. 

Come Down to Earth!

To climb down the tree, you must write the four-letter answer to each clue on the tree house planks. Change only one letter in each word as you go down!

1. **A _____ in the hand is worth two in the bush.**
2. **In a friendship try to be kind, since kindness is one of the ties that _____.**
3. **A strong _____ can force butterflies to the ground.**
4. **The magician waved her _____ and pulled a rabbit from a hat!**
5. **Lucy saw her baby sister in the hospital's maternity _____.**
6. **A promise means you've given your _____.**
7. **The early bird catches the _____.**

What is a puppy after it is five days old?
Six days old!

Wacky Words 1

Try to figure out these familiar animal words, phrases, and sayings from the way the words are arranged in the boxes below. The first one has been done for you.

1. hot dog

2. ______________

3. ______________

4. ______________

5. ______________

6. ______________

7. ______________

8. ______________

9. ______________

10. ____________________ 11. ____________________ 12. ____________________

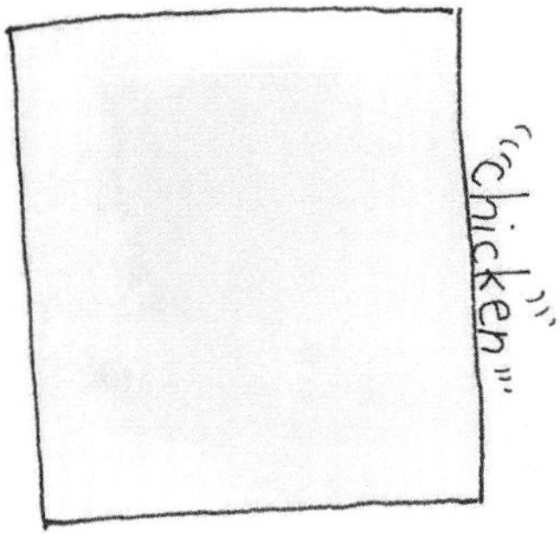

13. ____________________ 14. ____________________ 15. ____________________

16. ____________________ 17. ____________________ 18. ____________________

1. ______________ rat

Zoo Avenue

2. ______________ bunny

Write rhyming words to describe each animal that lives on Zoo Avenue. For example, the chatty cat is a "gabby tabby."

3. ______________ goose

4. ______________ eagle

5. ______________ mice
6. ______________ chick
7. ______________ duck
8. ______________ kitty
9. ______________ kangaroo
10. ______________ beaver

Unleash Me!

These dogs tangled their leashes chasing a goose through the park. To reveal what they're all thinking about now, follow each leash from a box to a dog, then write the letter you find next to that dog in the box.

Help Hulk!

Hulk swam to a diving platform in the pool but refuses to swim back, and Katie doesn't want to get wet! She found two boards $4\frac{1}{2}$ feet long, but the platform is 5 feet away from all sides. How can Katie use the boards to rescue Hulk without getting wet?

Hot Dogs

Each of the phrases below contains a word or expression that has a dog in it. Fill in the blanks with the correct answers. The first one has been done for you.

1. Pages torn or folded down in a book are  e a r e d

2. When you're feeling very ill, you're ____ __ _ 

3. One of the first swimming strokes you learn is the  _________

4. When you feel exhausted, you're  _____

5. A sign often posted by homeowners to warn intruders is __________ __ 

6. When it's pouring outside, it's ___________ _____ ____ 

Knot Likely?

Skippy wants to go for a walk, but his leash is a tangled mess. If you pull on the leash, two of the knots will tighten. Circle the one that will come undone.

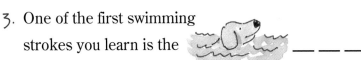

Those Crazy Cats!

The cat napping inside each answer below won't be much help, but the clues will! The first one has been done for you.

1. Cows

   c a t t l e

2. A little snooze

   __ __ __ __ __ __

3. A string game you play on your hands

   __ __ __'__ __ __ __ __ __ __

4. It turns into a butterfly

   __ __ __ __ __ __ __ __ __ __ __

5. A booklet listing things for sale

   __ __ __ __ __ __ __

6. Opposite of throw

   __ __ __ __ __

7. A reed with a furry brown top

   __ __ __ __ __ __ __

That Yarn Cat!

Knitty Kitty has four balls of yarn. How can she arrange them so that *each* ball of yarn touches the other three?

Cat's out of the Bag

The player who's forced to cross off the cat coming out of the bag loses!

The object of the game is to force your opponent to cross off the cat coming out of the sleeping bag. To start, player one crosses out as many bags as she wants in any *one* row. Player two can cross out more bags in the same row or choose another row. Players take turns until only the cat coming out of the bag remains. The player who must cross out this bag loses! Before you play, copy the page so you can play again.

Tiger by the Tail

Want a laugh? Just wait until you see your friends chasing their "tails." To play this game, the first girl in line must grab the handkerchief from the pocket of the last girl in line.

1. To begin, players hold on to the waist of the person in front of them. The last girl in line puts a handkerchief into her back pocket for the tail.
2. On "Go!" the girl in front runs and tries to snatch the tail, pulling the others along. To avoid being caught, the last girl wiggles her tail. Everyone else is caught in the middle!
3. When the girl in front catches the tail, she moves to the back of the line. The second person in line takes the lead and begins again.

What do you get when you cross a tiger with a canary?
I don't know, but when it sings you'd better listen!

Tail Endings

Add missing letters in front of the words below to make the name of an animal.
Note: Some words have more than one correct answer.

Examples: _m_ink, _tr_out

1. _________key
2. _________at
3. _________her
4. _________ark
5. _________imp
6. _________rot
7. _________rich
8. _________pine
9. _________use
10. _________ale

Triple-Tail Tag

The more players you have, the more fun this game will be. Choose two or three girls to be **It**. On "Go!" they each try to tag players. A tagged player gets in line behind the **It** who tagged her, holding her waist as they run to tag others. After everyone's caught, the **It** with the longest "tail" of players wins!

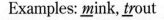

Peg's Ponies

Peg often mends her ponies' fences. To help her, arrange toothpicks in the following patterns for fences, then move them around to figure out the answers.

1. Wildfire broke a fence. Rearrange the 12 remaining toothpicks to make 6 triangular stalls.

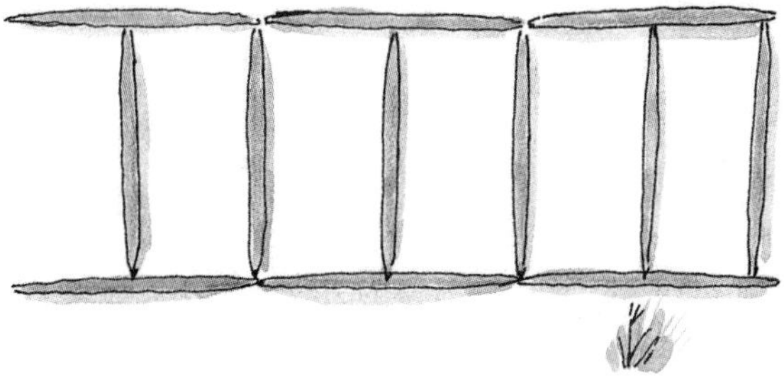

2. Peg just bought Trotter and needs another stall. Move 3 toothpicks to create 4 square stalls.

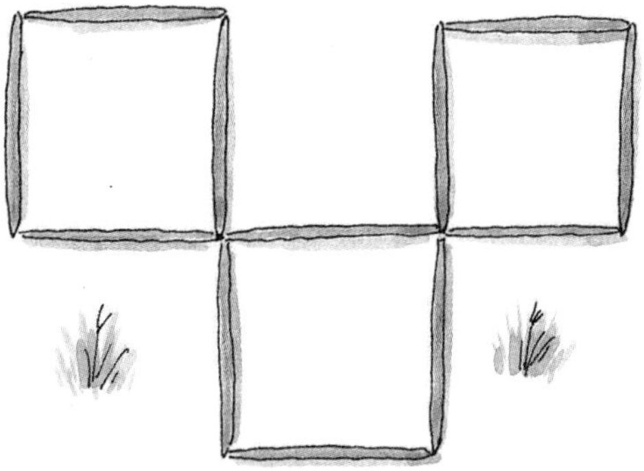

3. Peg wants her mare and foal to share a small stall and the other ponies to share a large stall. Remove just 8 toothpicks from the stalls at left to get one large square stall and one small square stall.

Mr. E. Mutt: Udder Chaos

Mr. E. Mutt has another case to solve. Farmer Fran contacted the pet detective and asked him, “What do you call it when two cows help each other?” Use the decoder below to find Mr. E.’s reply.

__ __ __ __ __ __ __ __ __ __ __ __

Cow-cu-late

How many triangles can you find on this cow?

Animazing Illusion

**What you see isn't necessarily what you get!
Try these optical illusions yourself—then share them with a friend.**

1. To see these lovebirds kiss, stare at a spot right between them. Now slowly bring the book toward your nose. Don't blink or adjust your vision. Smack!

2. Will the mountain goat reach the highest step on the mountain? Look carefully—these steps are playing tricks!

3. Point at a distant object. Close your right eye. Now open your right eye, and close your left. Did your finger move? Because our eyes are slightly spaced apart, they each see things in a slightly different way. Get the point?

Homeward Bound

Scout and Gypsy romped through the city all day. It seems they've strayed. Bring them home to their worried moms—to stay!

Creepy Cave

Not afraid of dark caves? Track down 17 cave-related words. Look forward, backward, upside down, or diagonally. Circle the words you find. The first one has been done for you.

Word Box

bats	bugs	creepy	dark	rats	spiders
bears	cave	crickets	eerie	rocks	water
beetles	cold	damp	mysterious	snakes	

M	Y	S	T	E	K	C	I	R	C
B	Y	S	P	E	R	S	T	A	R
E	L	S	P	R	A	C	V	A	E
A	O	W	T	I	D	E	C	B	E
R	C	S	W	E	D	C	O	U	P
S	O	E	I	A	R	E	R	G	Y
K	L	K	B	U	T	I	R	S	B
C	D	A	M	P	E	E	O	S	A
O	E	N	S	P	I	D	R	U	T
R	T	S	E	L	T	E	E	B	S

Avoid the Octopus

You can play this game all year—in leaves, snow, grass, or a pool!

To play, the Octopus swims in the "ocean," while the other players, who are Fish, line up on either side. When the Octopus shouts "Hungry!" everyone crosses to the other side of the ocean. Each player the Octopus tags becomes a tentacle. Each tentacle holds hands with the Octopus or another tentacle and helps her grab more Fish. The last Fish swimming wins!

Snake Eyes

Fool your friends with this hiss-terical feat!

While playing a game with dice, stop and tell your friends you can magically see through dice. To prove it, tell them the dice's facedown numbers. Here's how: The numbers on the opposite faces of a die always add up to 7. If a 4 shows, the opposite number is 3. If a 5 shows, the opposite number is 2. Roll the dice again to see if you still have the power. You will!

Farmyard Feed!

You'll need at least six players for this *moo*-velous game! While a helper hides peanuts in a designated "farmyard," players divide into teams of three or more. Each team picks a farmer to carry the bag and decides which animal to be—one team could be chickens, another cows.

On "Go!" everyone spreads out to search for peanuts. If a chicken finds a peanut, she clucks to alert the farmer. If a cow finds a peanut, she must moo. Only farmers can touch peanuts. Before long, the area will sound like a real farmyard! In the end, the team with the most peanuts wins.

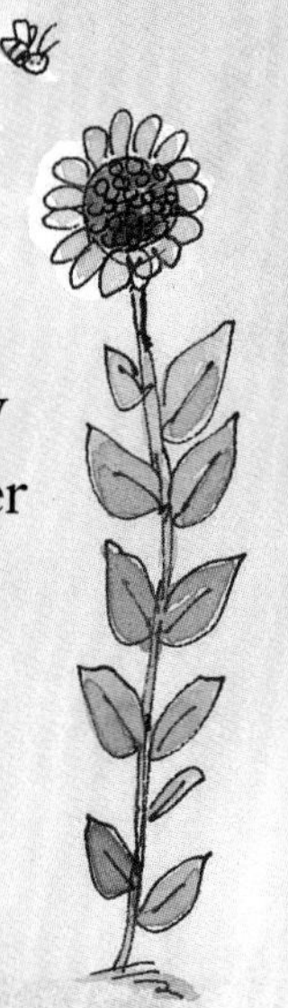

Ig-pay Atin-lay

Want to learn a language quickly? Try pig latin! To speak it, put the first letter of a word on the end of the word, and add an "ay" sound. Soon you won't have to think about how to do it! Say these sentences to a friend to see if she knows what you mean.

An-kay oo-yay alk-tay ig-pay atin-lay?

Oo-day oo-yay ont-way oo-tay earn-lay?

It-yay an-kay ee-bay our-yay
ecret-say anguage-lay!

Telephone Tune 1

If you have a touch-tone phone, call a friend who is *not* long-distance—or your parents won't be singing a happy tune. Ask your friend to listen as you press these buttons on your phone. Can she guess the tune?

6 6 6 7 8 8 7 (pause) 9 9 0 0 4

4 6 6 6 7 8 8 7 (pause) 9 9 0 0 4

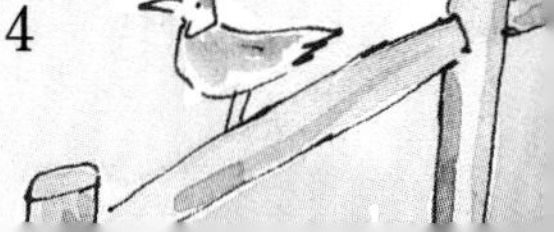

Jungle Books

The clues in this crossword are about some well-loved animal books.

Across

1. Chester travels by subway in a picnic basket in *A* _______ *in Times Square.*
5. Despite his mother's warnings, _______ Rabbit loses his blue coat in Mr. McGregor's garden.
6. Julie runs away from her Eskimo village and is befriended by _______.
8. This mouse is raised by human parents.
9. A young boy steals an abused beagle in _______.
13. A loyal family dog saves his master but gets rabies in *Old* _______.
14. In this touch-and-feel book, you can actually *Pat the* _______.
15. After a shipwreck, the Black _______ swims to an island.
16. *Where the Red* _______ *Grows* is about a boy's relationship with his coon dogs.

Down

1. George the monkey is very _______.
2. This comic-strip cat loves lasagna and torments Odie.
3. A girl lives alone for years in *Island of the Blue* _______.
4. To save Wilbur, Charlotte weaves messages in her _______.
7. A wild pony lives on an island in _______ *of Chincoteague.*
10. Calvin's comic-strip buddy who's a stuffed tiger
11. This *Wizard of Oz* character lacks courage.
12. He's a famous aardvark with a sister named D.W.

Word Box

Arthur	Garfield	Stallion
Bunny	Hobbes	Stuart Little
Cricket	lion	web
curious	Misty	wolves
Dolphins	Peter	Yeller
Fern	Shiloh	

1.
2.
3.
4.
5.
6.
7.
8.
9.
10.
11.
12.
13.
14.
15.
16.

Monarch Maze

When Monarch butterflies go south for the winter, they face many hardships—wind that blows them off course, birds that try to eat them, and cool weather that paralyzes them. Help these butterflies make it safely home.

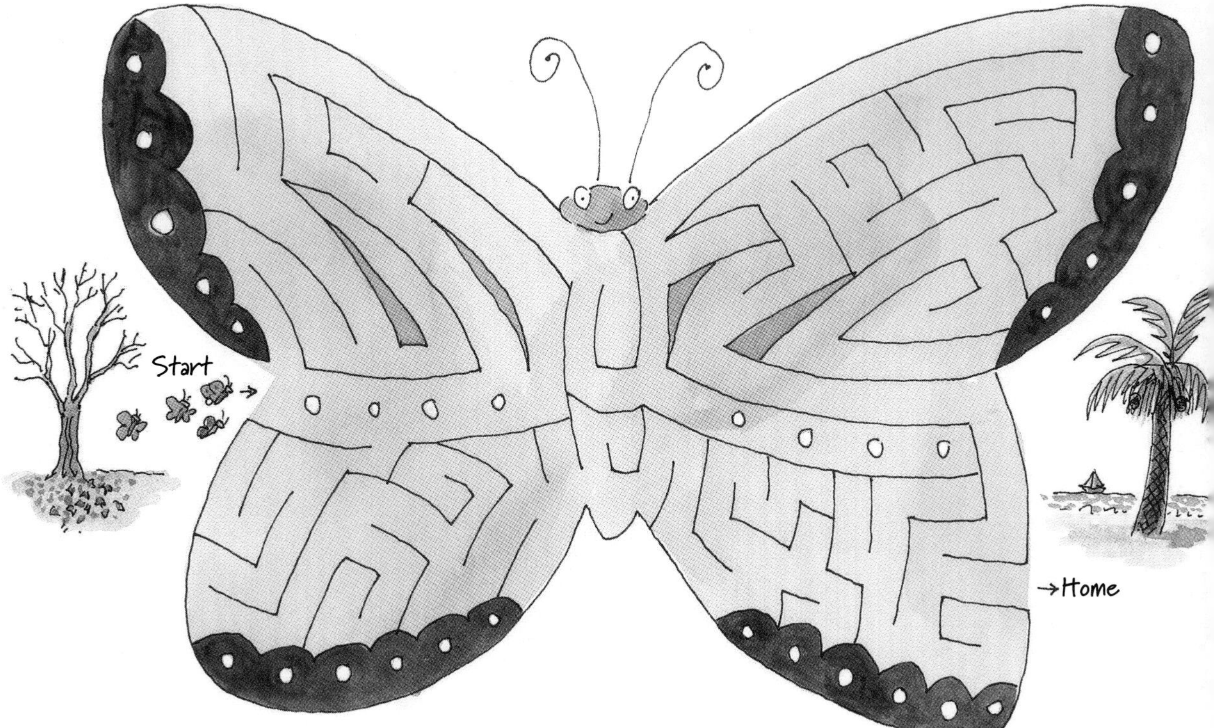

Match This Batch

Look at these two patterns on butterfly wings:

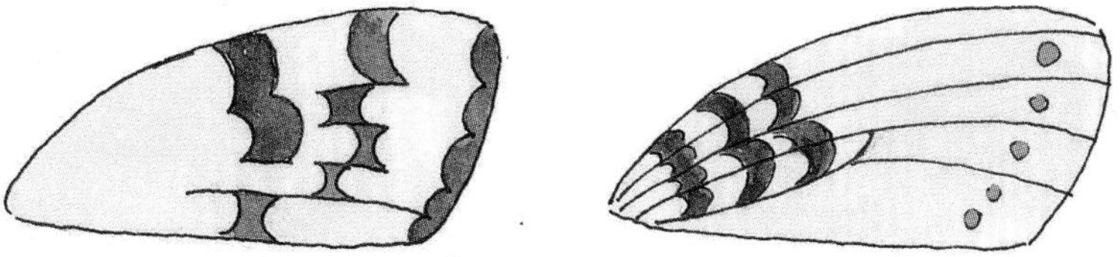

If you place the left wing, above, on top of the right wing, which of the patterns below would you see?

a.

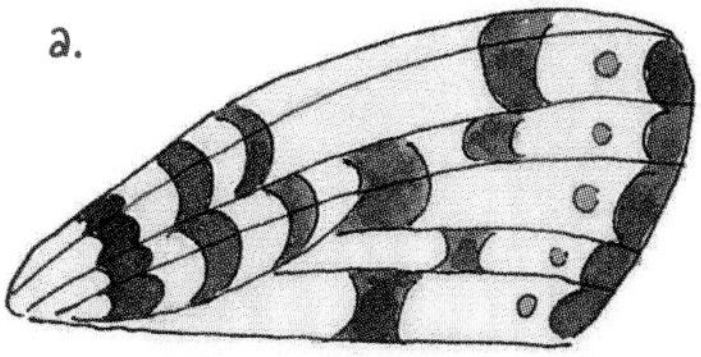

b.

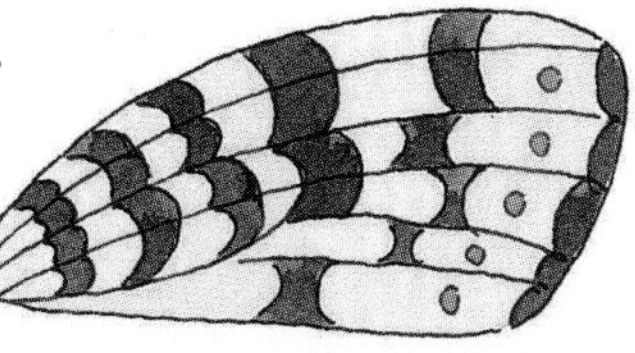

c.

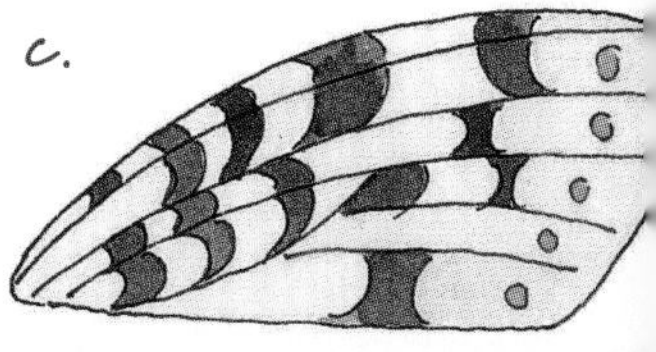

Get the Bugs Out!

No bugs are wanted in this game! Cross out all the B's, U's, and G's to discover a secret message hidden in the letters below.

W	B	A	L	G	K	U	O	B	N
T	H	U	E	W	G	I	B	L	D
G	S	I	B	U	G	D	B	U	E

Write the message here to find out what animal lovers like to do:

_ _ _ _   _ _   _ _ _   _ _ _ _ _   _ _ _ _

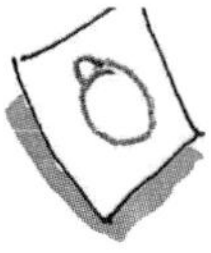

Ladybug, Ladybug...

Your goal is to fly away home—but you'll want to stick around and play this game again!

You'll need two dice, plus paper and pencil for each player. Each player picks a different number from 2 to 12. Take turns throwing the dice. Whenever a player's number is thrown, she gets to add a part of the ladybug to her picture, in this order:

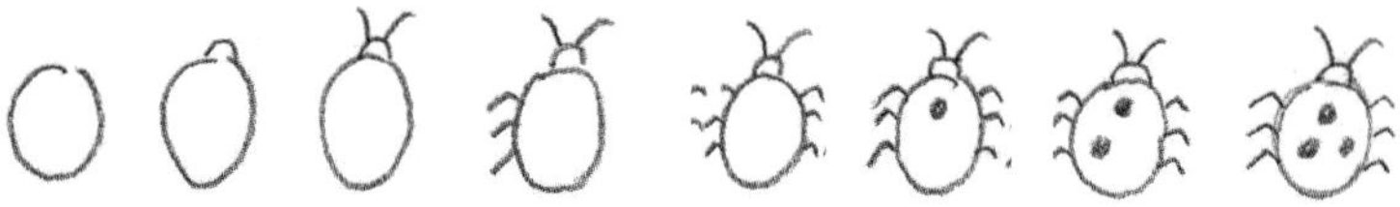

The first player to complete her ladybug wins!

A Bird in the Hand

In this game, if It spots a bird in your hand, your goose is cooked!

It stands inside the circle while players pass a badminton birdie behind their backs. When **It** spots the birdie, she points to the player who has it and yells "Bird!" That player instantly shows her hands. If she has the bird, she's **It**. If not, **It** tries two more times, then she's out of the game. To fool **It**, empty-handed players pretend to pass birdies. For extra fun, add more birdies!

Why are roosters the neatest birds?
Because they always carry their combs.

Bird Dog

The faster you play this game, the more fun you'll have! Everyone sits in a small circle of chairs. The Bird Dog stands in the middle. On "Go!" players begin tossing a badminton birdie to one another, trying to keep it from the Bird Dog's clutches. If the Bird Dog catches the birdie, the player who touched it last becomes the Bird Dog.

Shadow Hands

The Giggle Gang went wild making shadows on the wall. To see how they did it, ask a friend to hold a flashlight about 4 feet away from a plain wall in a dark room. Copy the positions shown with your hands. To make wings flap, ears wiggle, legs walk, or mouths open and close, just fiddle with fingers and hands. Practice, then put on a shadow show!

spider

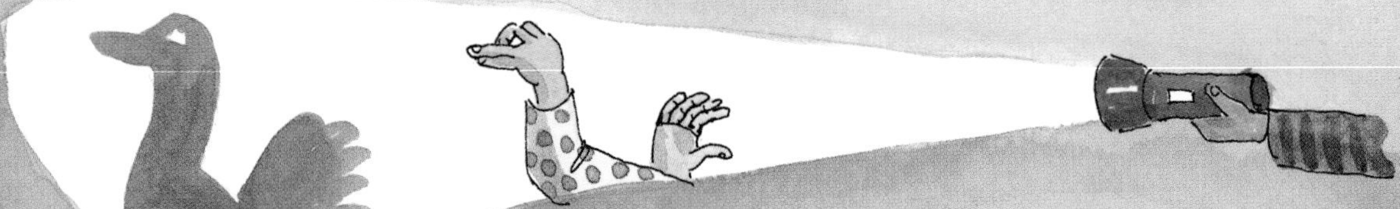

swan

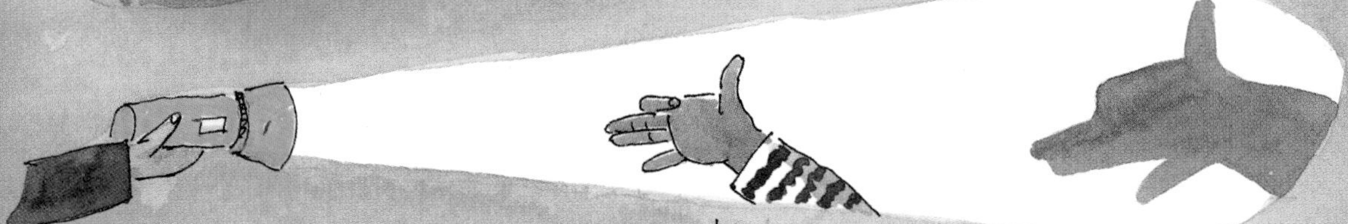

dog

elephant

rabbit

Coin Critters

Raid your piggy bank for art's sake. By tracing around a quarter, a dime, a nickel, and a penny, you can draw lots of animals! Practice drawing these, then create your own.

Set this butterfly free with a dime and a quarter.

Make this caterpillar inch along with a penny.

Bring this gator to life with a nickel.

Topsy Turtle

Arrange ten pennies like the ones on the turtle's shell. Then move just three coins to turn the shell upside down like this:

What's worse than a giraffe with a sore throat?

A turtle with claustrophobia!

Rebus Roundup

A *rebus* uses pictures and letters to make a word. See how well you can round up the critters in the rebuses below! Write the name of each clue in the blanks below its picture. Then add or subtract letters from the words you've written to find the answer.

1. 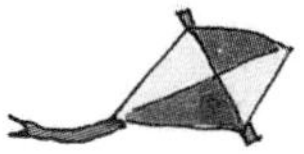 - E +  - T

___ ___ ___ ___   ___ ___ ___ ___

Answer: ___ ___ ___ ___ ___ ___

2.  - N  - DI + 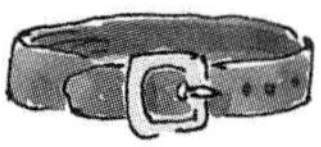 - BET

___ ___ ___   ___ ___ ___ ___   ___ ___ ___ ___

Answer: ___ ___ ___ ___ ___

3.  - GH + 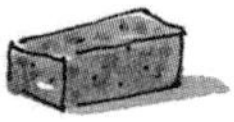 - BK + H

___ ___ ___ ___ ___   ___ ___ ___ ___ ___

Answer: ___ ___ ___ ___ ___ ___ ___

4.  - C +  - KE + T

___ ___ ___ ___   ___ ___ ___ ___

Answer: ___ ___ ___ ___ ___ ___

5. 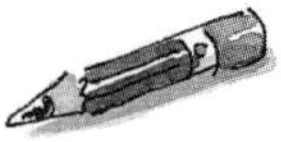 - CIL +  - M + 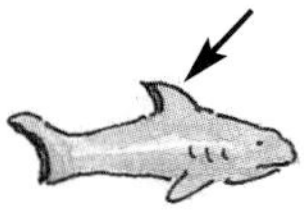 - F

___ ___ ___ ___ ___ ___   ___ ___ ___   ___ ___ ___

Answer: ___ ___ ___ ___ ___ ___ ___

Animal All-Ways

Never cross a kangaroo—unless you're playing this paper-and-pencil game!

Two players write the name of the same animal, such as *kangaroo,* in the middle of a piece of paper. Now they both create a mini crossword, adding as many words related to the animal as they can. The player with the most words wins!

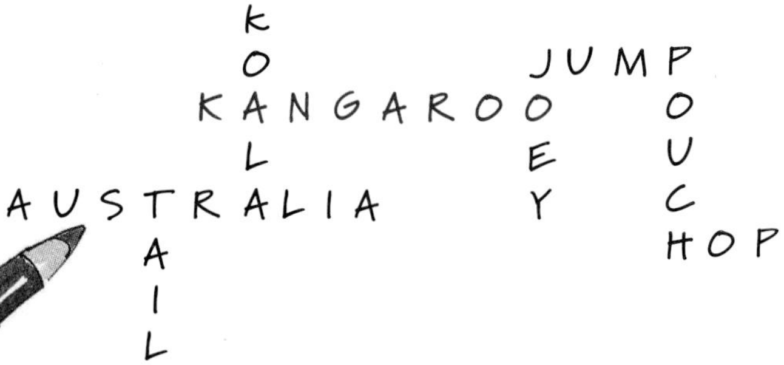

Try words from this list:

rhinoceros
chipmunk
chimpanzee
hippopotamus

Alpha-Pet Soup

To play, write each letter of the alphabet on a separate slip of paper. Mix up the slips in a bowl. Ask a player to draw out five letters, one at a time. Let's say she picks T B A D N. Each player writes a sentence about an animal using words that begin with those letters—in the order they were drawn. The player who finishes her sentence first wins that round.

Trained Bears Always Dance Nicely.

Top Pets

Ms. Fox came to class and found her list of the ten most popular pets had been scrambled. She figured out the first two, but was stumped by the rest. Help her unscramble the list.

1. cat
2. dog
3. ________________
4. ________________
5. ________________
6. ________________
7. ________________
8. ________________
9. ________________
10. ________________

Puzzling Pathways

Jenny lost her puppy, Clementine, in a park, and three of her friends are helping her search. Each girl can see only the intersections in a straight line down the paths in front of her. But one intersection is hidden from everyone's view. Of course, mischievous Clem is hiding there! Draw a picture of Clem at the only intersection no girl can see.

You're It!

Try out these animal rhymes when choosing who will be It in your next game.

Tarzan, Tarzan, in a tree,
Acting like a monkey!
Had no tail. Tarzan fell.
So long—farewell!

One, two, three,
Cindy caught a bumblebee!
Put it in her pouch,
Then sat on her couch.
Now out goes she.

(Use the name of the person you're pointing to in place of the name "Cindy.")

Bunny, bunny, soft and sweet,
Careful where you put your feet!
Lucky in a sock,
Lucky in a shoe.
Not so lucky is Y-O-U!

Acka backa
The duck's a quacker,
Acka backa boo!
If the duck's
a cracker smacker,
Out goes YOU!

Barnyard Babble

Did you hear that? Was it a bark or a bleat? A twitter or a tweet? Search this puzzle to find 26 animal sounds. You can form the words forward, backward, upside down, or diagonally. Circle the words you find.

Word Box

baa	buzz	coo	howl	oink	squeak
bark	caw	gobble	meow	peep	tweet
bleat	chirp	hiss	moo	quack	twitter
bray	cluck	honk	neigh	ribbit	whinny
		hoot	nicker		

G	O	B	B	L	E	S	N	E	I	G	H	C	H
O	I	K	A	E	L	M	S	P	V	O	I	N	O
B	N	N	D	W	H	I	N	N	Y	F	S	C	O
B	K	C	I	L	L	S	M	P	D	T	S	E	T
I	C	H	A	C	O	Q	U	E	H	O	W	L	W
Q	U	I	E	P	K	U	B	A	R	J	A	C	H
U	K	R	A	B	L	E	A	T	C	A	R	C	I
A	L	P	B	U	Z	A	R	J	I	F	E	F	N
C	H	I	R	Z	O	K	P	E	E	P	E	A	R
K	A	U	Q	Z	M	I	I	T	T	O	A	T	I
C	D	K	E	X	E	T	T	N	W	T	O	E	B
U	A	N	B	O	B	R	A	Y	O	S	I	E	B
L	M	O	O	O	A	R	H	U	E	L	F	W	I
C	A	H	O	C	A	W	O	T	M	U	S	T	T

What animal can jump higher than a barn?
Any animal. A barn can't jump!

Flights of Fancy

Birds of a feather stick together—sometimes in any mixed-up order. Unscramble these words to find 12 kinds of birds.

1. kawh ______________________
2. aglee ______________________
3. brion ______________________
4. danilacr ______________________
5. low ______________________
6. pinego ______________________
7. dmroickgnib ______________________
8. dinmhibumrg ______________________
9. pwsraro ______________________
10. sogoe ______________________
11. ubel ayj ______________________
12. rtapor ______________________

What do you get when you cross a centipede with a parrot?
A walkie-talkie!

For the Birds

To solve this puzzle circle the close-ups below that came from the larger picture at right.

a.

b.

c.

d.

e.

f.

g.

Duckling Dilemma

Ashley told her big sister Kim that she saw traffic stop for baby ducklings crossing the road.

"How many ducklings were there?" asked Kim, knowing Ashley hadn't learned all her numbers yet.

"Hmm," said Ashley. "One duckling was in front of two, one duckling was behind two, and one duckling was between two."

How many ducklings did Ashley see cross the road?

Letter Lunch

Chomp, a giant Panda from China, munched the sides off these bamboo letters. Add straight and diagonal lines to the munched-on letters to reveal three words that have an animal in them.

Mr. E. Mutt: Fat Cat

Smoky, a Dalmatian at the local fire department, was called to the scene after Socks ate the contents of a knitting bag. Mr. E. heard about the accident and dropped by. "What happens when a cat eats a ball of yarn?" Smoky asked Mr. E. Use this decoder to see Mr. E.'s reply.

On Thin Ice

Sitka loves practicing for the Alaskan Iditarod. She often leads her team over the frozen tundra, but a snowstorm has slowed her down. Help Sitka return home safely, then discover a design in the track she made on her trip.

Letters from Home

A mail sack delivered to Critter County Post Office fell onto the floor, causing six letters to slip out of their envelopes. Match each letter to its envelope.

1. It's been a while scents you've written to me, you stinker, so I figured I'd drop a line...

A. Ms. Flipper
C 1 Oceanside Lane

2. I wish you'd stop chewing the fat long enough to write! I spent most of the day in the kitchen bacon a cake.

B. Mr. Rattler
Desert Avenue, Apt. SSSS

3. I miss ewe so much. I was taking a baaath the other day and sang the song ewe used to sing to me. "I wish ewe were baaack from the fields..."

C. William Goat
888 Dump Road

A.____

B.____

C.____

D.____

E.____

F.____

D.
I. M. Porker
4 Sty Drive
5.
Jussst thought I'd let you know I've been rattling around in this old barn. I'm still grounded, but fang goodness I keep my spiritsss up...
4.
Water you doing? My porpoise for writing is to tell you that the crabs who lived next door have moved...
COFFEE
E.
P.U. Stinker
1 Smelly Street
6.
Billy, you can't keep horning in on other people's business. Now, stop it, kid! Just relax, comb your beard, and open up a tin can for dinner...
F.
USA
Baabs Woolworth
Gr-8 Meadow Way
FIRS
CLASS

Squishy Sardines

Be careful! The smaller the space, the louder the laughter in this hide-and-seek game. While **It** hides, players count to 25. Then all the players spread out to look for **It**. If you find **It**, shhh—keep the discovery a secret! Just squish into the hiding place with her. The last one to find the hiding place is the new **It**!

After a While, Crocodile

To play this version of tug-of-war, spread a sheet of newspaper on the floor. Then stand back quickly—if you fall into the "swamp," you'll be swallowed by a croc! Players hold hands around the newspaper. On "Go!" everyone pushes, pulls, squirms, and twists, trying to get others into the swamp. Can you stay out of the muck? Good luck!

Higher or Lower?

The numbers in the facts below are wrong—oops! Circle ↑ if you think the correct number is higher, and circle ↓ if you think the correct number is lower.

1. Cats have been pets for 500 years. ↑ ↓

2. A jellyfish is 80 percent water. ↑ ↓

3. An elephant drinks about 80 gallons of water a day. ↑ ↓

4. A lobster has 8 legs. ↑ ↓

5. A tortoise can reach a speed of 3 miles per hour. ↑ ↓

6. A slug has 100 teeth. ↑ ↓

7. The San Diego Zoo has 1,200 species—the largest collection of species in the United States. ↑ ↓

8. An adult porcupine has 20,000 quills. ↑ ↓

Tongue Twisters

Say the following four slick sentences at super speed!

Sweet sheep sleep soundly on shiny sheets.

Slick sharks keep score of shore scares.

A big black bear babbled to a bored bald bat till the bored bald bat bawled.

A weary hare wears heavy hairy ears.

Twisted Tunes

Can you guess the real names of these twisted rhymes and tunes?

1. **The Stuffed-Animals' Outdoor Feast**

   The Teddy Bears' Picnic

2. **Teeny-Tiny Arachnid**

3. **The Picnic Insects Go Walking in Formation, Individually**

4. **Madam Insect, Madam Insect, Flap Your Wings to Reach the Place You Live**

5. **This Petite Porker Visited the Food Store**

6. **I'm Carrying to My House an Infant Honey-Making Bug**

7. **To the Grocery, to the Grocery, to Purchase a Plump Porker**

8. **What Price Is the Pooch Behind the Pane of Glass?**

Telephone Tune 2

On a touch-tone phone, call a friend who is *not* long-distance and ask her to listen as you press these buttons on your phone. Can she name this tune?

6040666 (pause) 222 (pause) 666
6040666 (pause) 688684

Pig in a Poke

A pig in a poke is an old-fashioned expression that means you can't see what you're getting. The challenge of this game is to draw a pig—without being able to see it! Players wear blindfolds and draw pigs. Then everyone removes the blindfolds and votes on the best or funniest pig. The winner names the next animal for everyone to sketch.

Pig Out!

The goal: To be the first player to roll 100 points. The challenge: Not to be greedy!

To play, you'll need paper and a pencil for each player, and dice. A player rolls the dice and writes down her score. She can keep rolling and adding to her score, but if she rolls doubles, players shout "Pig Out!" She loses all the points she has earned on that turn. Take a chance, but don't be piggy! Pass the dice before it's too late.

Cold Hog Cash

Rachel has saved 40 cents. Make a list of every possible coin combination she can have in her bank if she has no pennies. If you find seven combinations, you're on the money!

Here's one of the seven possible combinations:

Pig Cushion

This game will liven up any *boar*-ing party! **It** wears a blindfold and sits with a small pillow or cushion on her lap. Everyone else sits around her. One by one, girls sit on her lap and say, "Oink!" **It** must guess which player is sitting on her lap. If she's right, they switch places. If not, the squeals go on!

Why shouldn't you tell a secret to a pig?
Because it's a squealer!

Creature Feature

Think twice before answering these brain benders.
They're not as easy as they seem.

1. If Digger digs a hole that is 4 feet wide by 4 feet long by 4 feet deep, how much dirt will he have in the hole?

2. Two mothers and two daughters went fishing. They were lucky. Each person caught a fish. Yet they had only three fish in the basket. Why was that?

3. Justina loves rodents. All her pets are gerbils except one, and all her pets are hamsters except one. How many gerbils and hamsters does she have?

4. Lucky wants to get into the carrot garden. If we know it takes two rabbits two days to dig two holes, how long will it take one rabbit to dig one hole?

Countin' Critters

Get your mental motor running with this tricky teaser.

As I was going to Saint Ives
I met a man with 7 wives.
Each wife had 7 sacks.
Each sack had 7 cats.
Each cat had 7 kits.
Kits, cats, sacks, wives—
How many were going to Saint Ives?

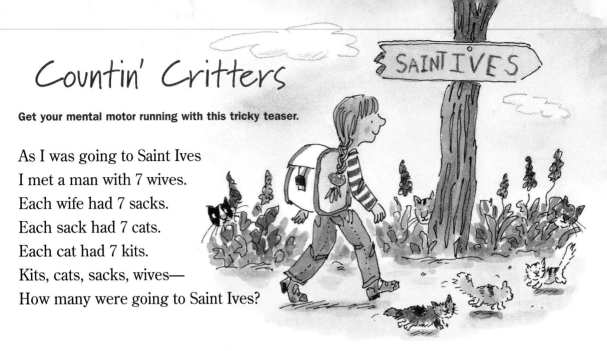

Mixed-Up Menagerie

Do you keep a lot of stuffed animals? If so, you have a menagerie! A *menagerie* is a collection of animals. You can also make a collection of words from the letters in the word *menagerie*. How many can you make? Find 10 and you're the cat's pajamas. Find 20 and you're a hot dog. Find 30 or more and you're as wise as an owl!

Wacky Words 2

Guess these familiar animal words, phrases, and sayings from the way the letters are arranged in the boxes below.

1. ______________ 2. ______________ 3. ______________

4. ______________ 5. ______________ 6. ______________

7. ______________ 8. ______________ 9. ______________

10. ______________ 11. ______________ 12. ______________

13. ______________ 14. ______________ 15. ______________

16. ______________ 17. ______________ 18. ______________

Elephant Chant

Try acting out this rhyme while you bounce a rubber ball.

1. I asked my mother
(stretch out your hand)

2. for fifty cents
(pretend to put money into your pocket)

3. to see the elephant
(make a trunk with your arm)

4. jump the fence.
(swing your leg over the ball)

5. She jumped so high
(jump into the air)

6. she touched the sky
(jump even higher)

7. and didn't get back
(touch your back)

8. till the Fourth of July.
(salute like a soldier)

Alpha-Pet Paragraph

Grab a friend and write a silly sentence about an animal using every letter of the alphabet. You may repeat letters, but they must be in order.

Here's ours!
A big-bellied cat devoured eight fat, fried, greasy hamburgers in Judy's kitchen, lazily licking, most noticeably, oily paws, quite relaxed, rested, so tired, uncoiled, visualizing wonderful wintry Xmas yummies, zzzzzzzz.

The Calico Cat

Play this game on car trips with family or friends.

Fill in the blanks of this phrase: "The calico cat is a ______ cat, and her name is ______." Words must begin with the same letter of the alphabet, starting with "A." So the first player might say, "The calico cat is an **a**ctive cat and her name is **A**nn." The other players must use different A words. On the next round, everyone uses "B" words, like "The calico cat is a **b**ashful cat and her name is **B**renda." Then use C, and so on. A player is out when she can't think of a word or repeats one already used. The last player left wins.

Monkeying Around

Every summer the Giggle Gang visits the monkey exhibit at the wild animal park. When they arrived this year, there was so much construction taking place they couldn't find their way. Draw a route around the construction site to the monkey exhibit.

Monkey See, Monkey Do

The object of this copycat game is to keep It from guessing who's the monkey.

1. Choose someone to be **It**. Ask her to leave the room while everyone else stands in a circle.
2. Pick a girl to be the Monkey. The Monkey starts an action, such as jumping on one leg or scratching her head. Everyone follows along.
3. Call **It** into the room, and ask her to stand in the circle. As the Monkey changes actions and everyone imitates her, **It** tries to guess who is the Monkey. If she guesses correctly, the Monkey becomes **It**. If she doesn't, after three tries she's out.

Tip: Don't watch the Monkey too closely, or you'll give her away!

Join the Club!

As soon as a few of the animals saw the clubhouse names, they realized they were in the wrong line. Cross off one animal in each line that decided not to join.

1. **The members of this club like to live in the mountains.**

2. **The members of this club like to come out at night.**

3. **The members of this club are equipped with scent glands.**

4. The members of this club have babies called calves.

5. The members of this club can live longer than 50 years.

6. The members of this club like to hibernate.

Camouflaged Critters

Inside each sentence you'll find a hidden animal waiting to be discovered. Draw a box around it when you find it. If you need help, check the Word Box. To get you started, the first one has been done for you.

Word Box

beaver	goat	ostrich
weasel	seal	otter

1. The movie about the robot got terrible reviews.
2. Hannah's favorite book is about a lost rich girl.
3. Margo attached a sign to the door saying "Come in!"
4. The colorful sailboats on the sea looked beautiful.
5. Gabe averages five trips to the library a month.
6. Jellybean wrapped herself around a leg of Jean's new easel.

Mr. E. Mutt: Bad Weather

Mr. E. and Rita Raccoon were watching Merryweather Weasel's weather report, when she announced, "Tonight it's going to rain cats and dogs!"

"What should we do?" asked Rita. Use the umbrella decoder to see Mr. E.'s reply.

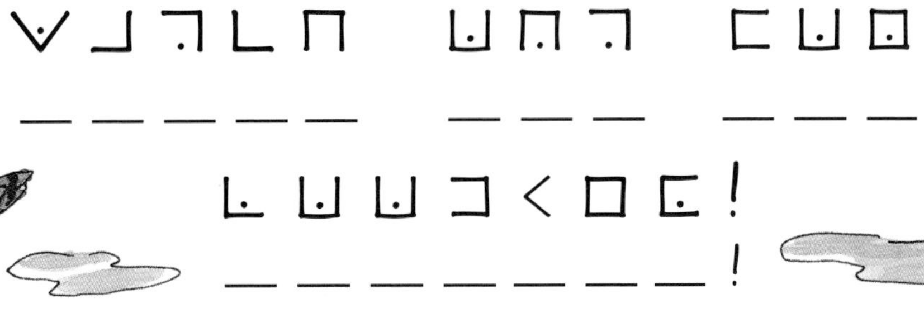

Den Again

A pack of hounds chased Rose and her neighbors into a nearby field. The hounds have left, but the foxes can't find their dens. Draw a path from each fox to its den without crossing another fox's path or going outside the wall.

Baby Boom

You know that a chick is a baby chicken and a calf is a baby cow, but did you know that a chick is also a baby penguin and a calf is a baby giraffe? To solve this puzzle, draw lines across the list to match the baby to the adult, then circle the baby animals in the word search. They may be spelled forward, backward, upside down, or diagonally.

P	I	R	E	A	G	L	E	T	J	B	M	A	L
C	U	B	H	K	O	Y	B	A	R	O	Y	R	N
M	I	K	U	I	O	E	H	S	A	P	O	I	J
K	O	B	N	T	E	L	G	I	P	N	L	O	K
A	I	W	T	T	R	H	U	U	D	N	E	I	M
X	A	D	E	E	O	S	P	A	C	X	T	O	C
D	V	K	R	G	I	A	A	U	M	T	N	V	Y
F	A	W	M	O	N	P	D	D	E	O	O	F	G
N	N	F	H	S	U	I	C	N	N	I	M	O	N
W	I	Y	A	L	J	G	L	E	A	A	G	A	E
A	T	J	N	I	A	L	L	K	E	G	R	L	T
F	S	O	N	N	B	E	L	R	C	N	N	A	S
O	U	E	A	G	A	M	D	A	D	U	E	A	M
T	J	Y	H	M	C	H	I	C	K	A	D	R	K

Dirt Dodgers

In the blanks below, write each letter in the order you cross it while going through the maze. If you solve the maze correctly, you'll discover a gopher's favorite thing to do.

_ _ _ _ _

_ _ _

_ _ _ _ _ _ _ _ _ _!

Twisted Tales

Can you guess the titles of these well-known stories?

1. **Yellow Hair and the Four-Minus-One Grown-Up Cubs**

 ____

2. **Step Aside for Young Quackers**

 ____

3. **The King of the Jungle, the Woman Who Casts Spells, and the Closet**

 ____

4. **Ebony Pretty One**

 ____

5. **Wee Scottish Girl, Return to Your House**

 ____

Letter Play

To unscramble this word, first copy these letters onto small squares of paper.

L W E A U

Now move the paper squares around until you spell the name of a desert animal.

Horsing Around

Saddle up this puzzle, and you'll find 25 horse-related words. Look forward, backward, upside down, or diagonally to find each word. Then circle the words you find.

A	S	O	R	X	R	E	T	D	B	R	A	N	T
S	T	A	L	L	E	M	M	W	D	A	I	R	E
B	I	T	Z	A	I	O	O	A	A	I	Q	G	K
L	R	S	C	T	N	L	N	L	D	T	J	A	N
A	R	J	A	S	S	A	D	K	A	O	I	L	A
N	U	O	N	J	B	R	U	S	H	S	M	L	L
K	P	H	T	O	R	M	R	O	S	A	S	O	B
E	S	N	E	E	I	B	O	K	A	D	L	E	E
G	K	E	R	O	D	J	R	C	E	D	O	T	S
R	S	A	D	D	L	E	B	A	Y	A	H	N	T
A	H	A	R	N	E	S	S	T	D	R	T	O	R
I	O	B	O	F	R	D	Y	R	X	V	R	M	A
N	E	R	A	G	A	L	L	O	P	T	I	U	W
R	S	E	S	S	A	L	O	M	M	J	G	M	C

Word Box

bay	brush	girth	oats	stirrups
bit	canter	grain	reins	straw
blanket	currycomb	harness	saddle	tack
bran	dam	hay	shoes	trot
bridle	gallop	molasses	stall	walk

Horse Sense

1. Three members of the Giggle Gang created the Nifty Fifty Club because the numbers on their jerseys totaled 50. Circle the girls above in the club.

2. Samantha has 15 horses. All but 8 of them have won competitions. How many horses have not won? ________

3. Tammy rode to Tulsa on Tuesday, stayed two nights, and returned on Tuesday. How did Tammy do this? ________________________________

4. Three of Greta's horses compete in jumping events, and four of her horses compete in dressage. What's the smallest number of horses Greta could own? ________

5. Champ nibbled on the homework Helen had in her back pocket. Replace the plus and minus symbols Champ ate to make Helen's answers correct.

8 1 3 = 6 3 7 4 2 = 4

5 2 2 3 = 6 9 1 7 7 = 8

Teddy Bear, Teddy Bear

This traditional rhyme is still a favorite when jumping rope! Try it with your friends. Rope turners say the rhyme while the jumper acts it out.

Teddy bear, teddy bear, turn around.
Teddy bear, teddy bear, touch the ground.
Teddy bear, teddy bear, read the news.
Teddy bear, teddy bear, shine your shoes.
Teddy bear, teddy bear, go upstairs.
Teddy bear, teddy bear, say your prayers.
Teddy bear, teddy bear, turn out the light.
Teddy bear, teddy bear, say good night!

Switch places with a rope turner, and begin again.

Bouncing Bears

Turners have as much fun as jumpers with this jump-rope jamboree!

Jumper hops into the twirling rope and says: "Hello, hello, hello, sir."

Turners say: "Meet me at the grocer."

Jumper: "No, sir."

Turners: "Why, sir?"

Jumper: "Because I have a cold, sir."

Turners: "Where'd you get the cold, sir?"

Jumper: "At the North Pole, sir."

Turners: "What'cha doing there, sir?"

Jumper: "Catching Polar bears, sir."

Turners: "How many did you catch, sir?"

Jumper counts and jumps fast on red hot peppers until she is out: "1 sir, 2 sir..."

The girl with the most jumps is the Bouncing Bear Princess!

What did the teddy bear say
when asked if she wanted dessert?
"No thanks! I'm stuffed."

Annie's Poodle

Can your friends guess what Annie's poodle likes? Feed them clues. For instance, Annie's poodle likes kittens but not cats. If someone asks, "Does Annie's poodle like cake?" you say, "No, Annie's poodle doesn't like cake, she likes cookies." Keep playing until everyone's figured out the secret: Annie's poodle likes only words with double letters.

Other clues you can give:

Annie's poodle likes puzzles but not games.
Annie's poodle likes pizza but not pretzels.
Annie's poodle likes grass but not flowers.

Poodle Parlor

Things took a wrong turn when Precious went to the Poodle Parlor. Number these boxes in the correct order to see what happened.

Houdini's Great Escape

Mindy named her guinea pig Houdini because of his great escapes. He escaped again last night! Carefully study the missing guinea pig poster Mindy drew, then turn the page.

Missing
Houdini
call
555-1234

Houdini's Great Escape!

Houdini wasn't the only guinea pig that escaped from his cage last night.
Rodent Recovery rounded up eight of them!
Based on the poster from the previous page, find Houdini. Don't look back!

Paw-sible Solutions

Fill in the empty boxes with these animal tracks:

No track can appear more than once in each row or column.

Water World

While at Water World, the gang discovered a tank filled with wacky creatures. For example, a catfish looked like a cat with fins. Can you name 12 others?

Walk on the Wild Side

See if you can solve this crossword without peeking at the Word Box!

Across

1. A huge gray beast that wallows in mud to stay cool (shortened name)
4. This animal's trunk is actually a long nose with a lip.
8. Eeyore might not agree, but people often think this animal is stupid.
9. Small animals rest inside this part of a fallen tree.
10. This poisonous snake isn't a baby, but it carries a baby's toy.
12. Large flightless bird
13. Never fool with Mother ______!
16. The sounds pigs make
18. The fabled number of lives a cat has
20. Tarzan's ape-like companion was this kind of animal.
23. To lay their eggs, salmon swim up a _____.
26. This member of the deer family has very large antlers.
27. Noah put two of each animal on the ark because of a ______.
28. King of the jungle
29. To communicate, a lion ______.
30. The part of a plant below ground that some animals eat
31. A ______lion lives in the Pacific Ocean.

Down

1. Despite these spiny-haired animals' names, they aren't related to pigs.
2. A bird that looks like it wears a tuxedo
3. Gray whales are at home in the ______.
4. Some kinds of this snake-like fish can shock prey with electricity.
5. The U.S. national bird
6. This fast runner couldn't beat the tortoise in a race.
7. Many wild animals in the U.S. are protected in a ______ ______.
11. A large kind of deer
14. A gorilla
15. This animal looks like it wears a mask.
17. A spirited horse; a trusty ______, indeed!
19. This arctic country is home to reindeer.
21. Some animals eat ______, especially anteaters.
22. Wild animals are often displayed in a ______.
24. All mammals need to breathe ______.
25. A plant that covers damp rocks and is a home to some insects and spiders

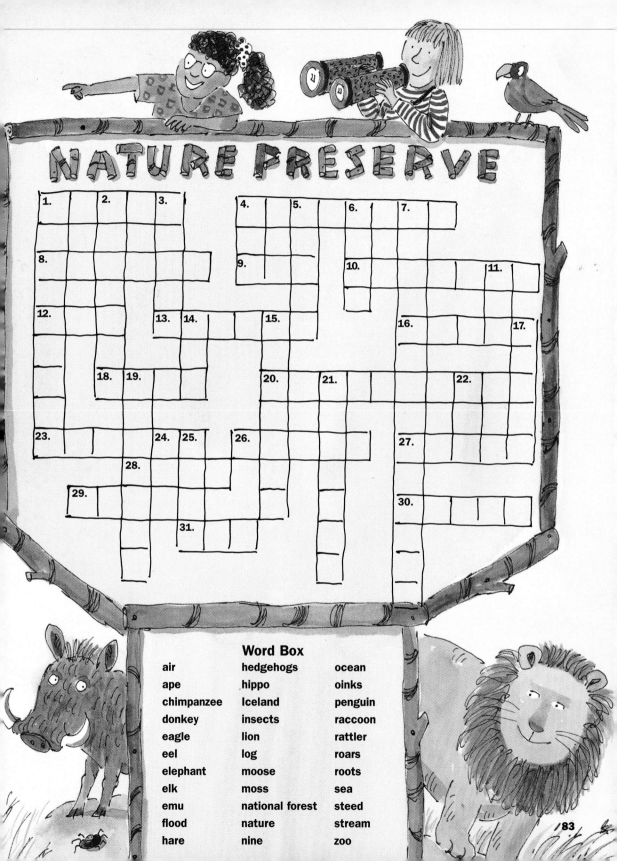

NATURE PRESERVE

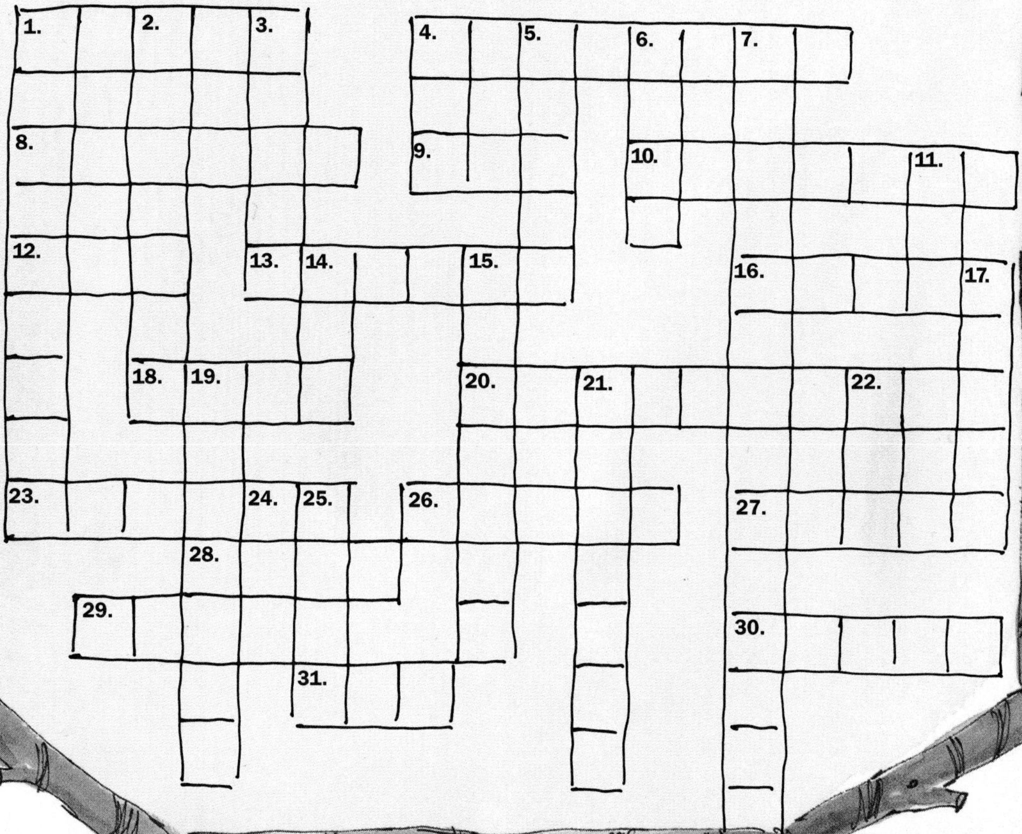

Word Box

air	hedgehogs	ocean
ape	hippo	oinks
chimpanzee	Iceland	penguin
donkey	insects	raccoon
eagle	lion	rattler
eel	log	roars
elephant	moose	roots
elk	moss	sea
emu	national forest	steed
flood	nature	stream
hare	nine	zoo

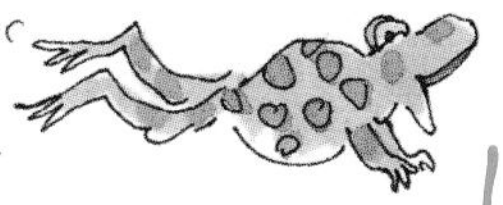

Leap, Frog!

The Giggle Gang held a frog-jumping contest. To see what order the frogs finished in (first through fourth place) read the clues. Write “no” in the square on the scorecard when a frog cannot take that place. Write “yes” in the square when it can.We did the first one for you.

CLUES

1. Croakie was ahead of Ribbit.
2. Ribbit was ahead of Bull.
3. Peeper was ahead of Croakie.

Hint: You may need to reread the clues.

	1st	2nd	3rd	4th
Ribbit	NO			
Croakie				NO
Peeper				
Bull				

First ______________

Second ______________

Third ______________

Fourth ______________

Pet Patrol

Merry Mouse moved into a new attic and decided to throw a dinner party. When 28 uninvited guests showed up—dogs, cats (yikes!), and other pets—Merry called the Pet Patrol. Help the patrol round up the uninvited guests. Form words forward, backward, upside down, and diagonally.

R	O	M	D	A	L	M	A	T	I	A	N	O	T
A	S	A	A	F	T	O	S	I	A	M	E	S	E
H	L	N	C	I	F	I	G	H	L	U	R	H	R
A	E	X	H	S	N	P	B	B	K	T	A	O	R
M	A	I	S	H	O	E	I	B	F	T	B	R	I
S	B	E	H	J	B	R	C	P	A	E	Y	T	E
T	G	I	U	O	D	S	D	O	B	R	S	H	R
E	I	L	N	E	R	I	X	N	O	O	S	A	E
R	P	L	D	B	E	A	G	L	E	N	I	I	S
C	A	O	S	I	A	N	E	S	U	E	N	R	E
O	E	C	T	O	R	R	A	P	O	B	I	E	G
L	N	R	E	T	R	I	E	V	E	R	A	S	N
L	I	E	L	A	B	A	P	E	R	S	N	R	I
Y	U	X	L	B	X	O	D	A	L	M	A	O	K
M	G	O	A	B	N	T	E	R	R	E	F	H	E
A	N	B	H	Y	H	O	R	E	L	D	O	O	P

Word Box

Abyssinian	Dalmatian	Lab	Persian	shorthair
beagle	ferret	Maine coon	pony	Siamese
bird	fish	Manx	poodle	tabby
boxer	guinea pig	mutt	rabbit	terrier
collie	hamster	parrot	retriever	
dachshund	horse	Pekingese	rex	

Kitty City

The cats shown at left had their pictures taken this morning. Can you find these cats around Kitty City now?

Tom

Allie

Cathy

Tony

AG
FIRE STATION
KITTY'S
FISH SHOP
STOP
GUARD

Answers

Page 6

Purr-fect Pet Show

1. three
2. orange, blue, and red
3. a carrot
4. pigs
5. a sign
6. a dollhouse
7. brushing her teeth
8. a skunk

Mr. E. Mutt: Owl Ouch

She doesn't give a hoot!

Page 7

Picture This

Pages 8–9

Teacher's Pet

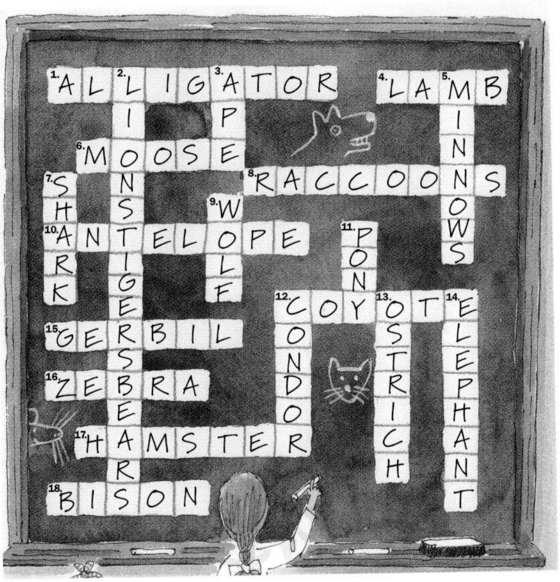

Page 10

Cross-Outs

A Mouse On Vacation

Page 11

Sea Things

sand	seaweed	starfish
sand dollar	shark	stingray
school of fish	shell	striped fish
sea lion	snail	swimmers
sea snake	snorkels	swimsuits
sea turtle	sponge	swordfish
seahorse	squid	

Page 12

Two of a Kind

Page 13

Come Down to Earth!

1. bird
2. bind
3. wind
4. wand
5. ward
6. word
7. worm

Pages 14–15

Wacky Words 1

1. hot dog
2. hammerhead shark
3. *Goldilocks and the Three Bears*
4. frog in the throat
5. *One Fish, Two Fish, Red Fish, Blue Fish*
6. leapin' lizards
7. puppy love
8. birdcage
9. butterfly
10. top dog
11. horsefly
12. goosebumps
13. chicken out
14. electric eel
15. rugrat
16. ants in the pants
17. blue jay
18. fishhook

Pages 16–17

Zoo Avenue

1. fat rat
2. funny bunny
3. loose goose
4. legal eagle
5. nice mice
6. sick chick
7. stuck duck
8. pretty kitty
9. blue kangaroo
10. weaver beaver

Page 18

Unleash Me!

A Wild-Goose Chase!

Help Hulk!

Page 19

Hot Dogs

1. dog-eared
2. sick as a dog
3. dog paddle
4. dog tired
5. beware of dog
6. raining cats and dogs

Knot Likely?

A and B will tighten. C will come undone.

Page 20

Those Crazy Cats!

1. cattle
2. catnap
3. cat's cradle
4. caterpillar
5. catalog
6. catch
7. cattail

That Yarn Cat!

Page 23

Tail Endings

Possible answers:

1. donkey, monkey, turkey
2. bat, cat, rat, goat, muskrat
3. panther, gopher
4. shark, aardvark, lark
5. chimp
6. parrot
7. ostrich
8. porcupine
9. mouse, grouse
10. whale

Page 24

Peg's Ponies

1. 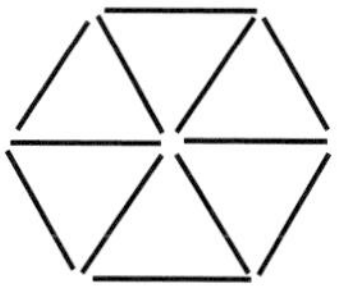

2. 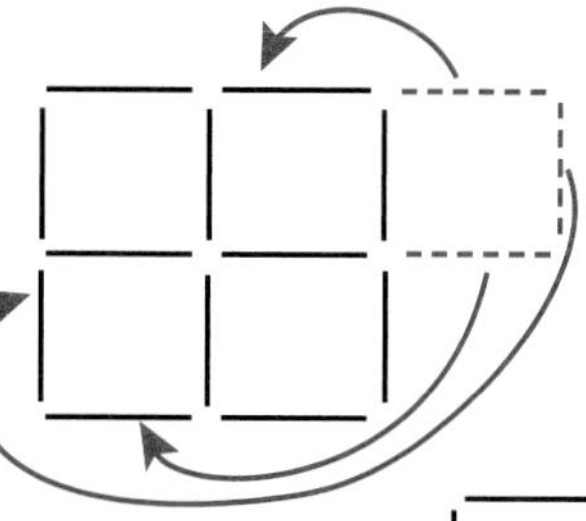

3. 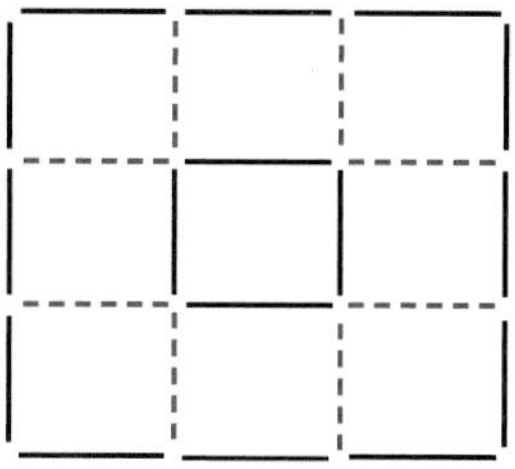

Page 25

Mr. E. Mutt: Udder Chaos

Cowoperation

Cow-cu-late

46

Page 27

Homeward Bound

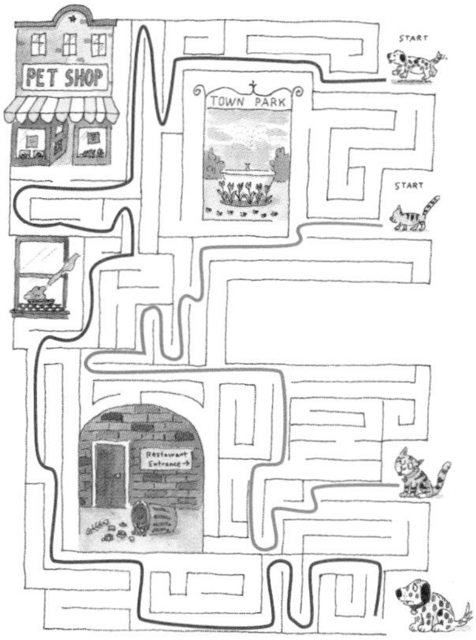

Page 28

Creepy Cave

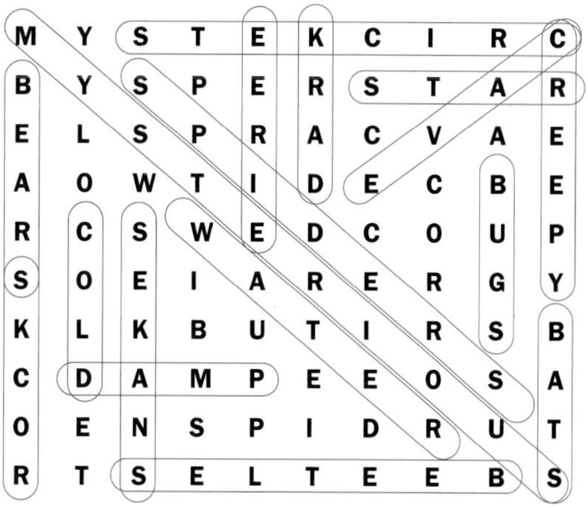

Page 31

Ig-pay Atin-lay

Can you talk pig latin? Do you want to learn? It can be our secret language!

Telephone Tune 1

"Old MacDonald Had a Farm"

Pages 32–33

Jungle Books

Page 34

Monarch Maze

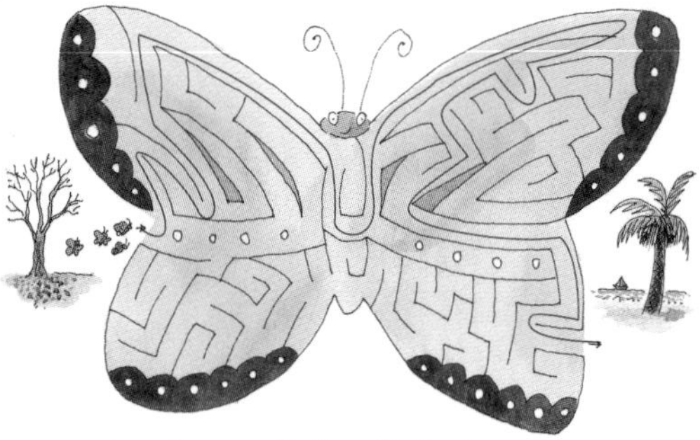

Match This Batch

b.

Page 35

Get the Bugs Out!

Walk on the wild side

Page 38

Topsy Turtle

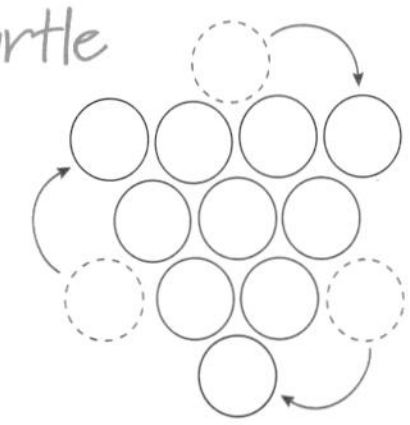

Page 39

Rebus Roundup

1. kitten
2. camel
3. ostrich
4. rabbit
5. penguin

Page 41

Top Pets

3. rabbit
4. snake
5. horse
6. fish
7. bird
8. hamster
9. ferret
10. guinea pig

Page 42

Puzzling Pathways

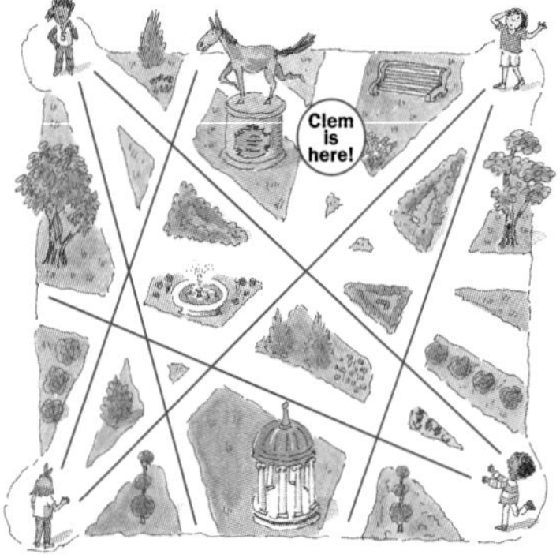

Pages 44–45

Barnyard Babble

G	O	B	B	L	E	S	N	E	I	G	H	C	H
O	I	K	A	E	L	M	S	P	V	O	I	N	O
B	N	N	D	W	H	I	N	N	Y	F	S	C	O
B	K	C	I	L	L	S	M	P	D	T	S	E	T
I	C	H	A	C	O	Q	U	E	H	O	W	L	W
Q	U	I	E	P	K	U	B	A	R	J	A	C	H
U	K	R	A	B	L	E	A	T	C	A	R	C	I
A	L	P	B	U	Z	A	R	J	I	F	E	F	N
C	H	I	R	Z	O	K	P	E	E	P	E	A	R
K	A	U	Q	Z	M	I	I	T	T	O	A	T	I
C	D	K	E	X	E	T	T	N	W	T	O	E	B
U	A	N	B	O	B	R	A	Y	O	S	I	E	B
L	M	O	O	O	A	R	H	U	E	L	F	W	I
C	A	H	O	C	A	W	O	T	M	U	S	T	T

Page 46

Flights of Fancy

1. hawk
2. eagle
3. robin
4. cardinal
5. owl
6. pigeon
7. mockingbird
8. hummingbird
9. sparrow
10. goose
11. blue jay
12. parrot

Page 47

For the Birds

d, e, and f

Duckling Dilemma

3 ducklings

Page 48

Letter Lunch

PIGPEN

PONYTAIL

COWGIRL

Mr. E. Mutt: Fat Cat

She has mittens.

Page 49

On Thin Ice

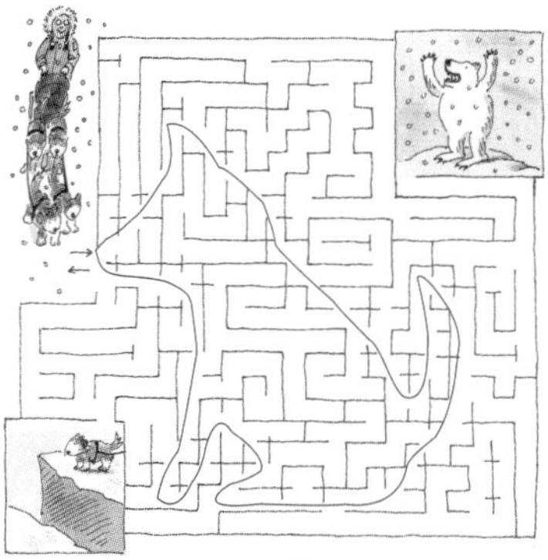

Pages 50–51

Letters from Home

A. 4 C. 6 E. 1

B. 5 D. 2 F. 3

Pages 53

Higher or Lower?

1. (↑) ↓ Scientists believe cats began to live with people about 5,000 years ago!
2. (↑) ↓ A jellyfish is 95 percent water.
3. ↑ (↓) An elephant drinks about 50 gallons of water a day.
4. (↑) ↓ A lobster has 10 legs.
5. ↑ (↓) A tortoise travels only .03 miles per hour.
6. (↑) ↓ Slugs have about 27,000 teeth on their tongues.
7. ↑ (↓) The San Diego Zoo has about 800 species of animals—the largest in the U.S.
8. (↑) ↓ An adult porcupine has more than 30,000 quills.

Page 55

Twisted Tunes

2. "Eensy, Weensy Spider"
3. "The Ants Go Marching One by One"
4. "Ladybug, Ladybug, Fly Away Home"
5. "This Little Piggy Went to Market"
6. "I'm Bringing Home a Baby Bumblebee"
7. "To Market, to Market, to Buy a Fat Pig"
8. "How Much Is That Doggie in the Window?"

Page 55 (cont.)

Telephone Tune 2

"Mary Had a Little Lamb"

Page 57

Cold Hog Cash

1. 1 quarter, 1 dime, 1 nickel
2. 1 quarter, 3 nickels
3. 4 dimes
4. 3 dimes, 2 nickels
5. 2 dimes, 4 nickels
6. 1 dime, 6 nickels
7. 8 nickels

Page 58

Creature Feature

1. None. There is no dirt in a hole.
2. One was a grandmother, one a mother, and one a daughter.
3. Two. Justina has one of each.
4. Each rabbit takes two days to dig a hole, so it'll take Lucky two days.

Page 59

Countin' Critters

Just one! Everyone else was heading in the opposite direction.

Mixed-Up Menagerie

aerie, age, agree, aim, air, am, amen, an, anger, are, arm, eager, ear, earn, eerie, gain, game, gear, gee, gem, genie, germ, germane, gin, grain, gram, green, grim, grime, grin, in, main, man, mane, manger, mar, mare, margin, marine, me, meager, mean, meaner, men, mere, merge, mine, miner, nag, name, near, rag, rage, rain, ram, ran, rang, range, ream, regain, reign, rein, remain, rename, renege, rig, rim, ring

Pages 60–61

Wacky Words 2

1. red-headed woodpecker
2. piggybank
3. firefly
4. greyhound
5. *Black Beauty*
6. tuna fish sandwich
7. cowgirl
8. grasshopper
9. piggy back
10. dragonfly
11. monkeying around
12. starfish
13. The cow jumped over the moon.
14. pigtail
15. *The Cat in the Hat*
16. mountain goats
17. *Rockin' Robin*
18. snowy owl

Page 64

Monkeying Around

Pages 66–67

Join the Club!

1. camel
2. ostrich
3. pig
4. deer
5. squirrel
6. otter

Page 68

Camouflaged Critters

2. Hannah's favorite book is about a lost rich girl.
3. Margo attached a sign to the door saying "Come in!"
4. The colorful sailboats on the sea looked beautiful.
5. Gabe averages five trips to the library a month.
6. Jellybean wrapped herself around a leg of Jean's new easel.

Mr. E. Mutt: Bad Weather

Watch out for poodles!

Page 69

Den Again

Page 70–71

Baby Boom

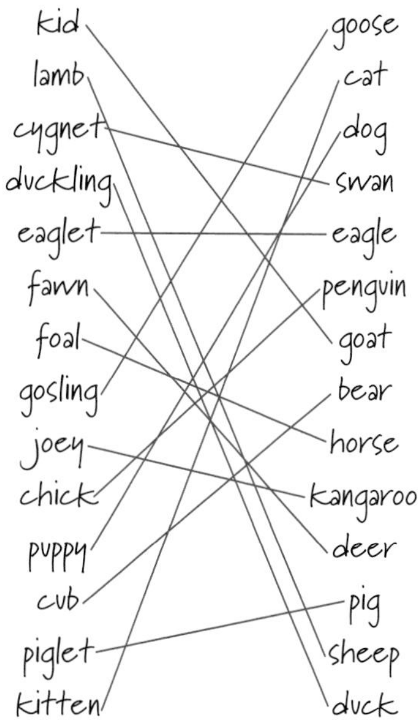

Page 70–71 (cont.)

Baby Boom (cont.)

P	I	R	E	A	G	L	E	T	J	B	M	A	L
C	U	B	H	K	O	Y	B	A	R	O	Y	R	N
M	I	K	U	I	O	E	H	S	A	P	O	I	J
K	O	B	N	T	E	L	G	I	P	N	L	O	K
A	I	W	T	T	R	H	U	U	D	N	E	I	M
X	A	D	E	E	O	S	P	A	C	X	T	O	C
D	V	K	R	G	I	A	A	U	M	T	N	V	Y
F	A	W	M	O	N	P	D	D	E	O	O	F	G
N	N	F	H	S	U	I	C	N	N	I	M	O	N
W	I	Y	A	L	J	G	L	E	A	A	G	A	E
A	T	J	N	I	A	L	L	K	E	G	R	L	T
F	S	O	N	N	B	E	L	R	C	N	N	A	S
O	U	E	A	G	A	M	D	A	D	U	E	A	M
T	J	Y	H	M	C	H	I	C	K	A	D	R	K

Page 72

Dirt Dodgers

Page 73

Twisted Tales

1. *Goldilocks and the Three Bears*
2. *Make Way for Ducklings*
3. *The Lion, the Witch, and the Wardrobe*
4. *Black Beauty*
5. *Lassie, Come Home*

Letter Play

C A M E L

Page 74

Horsing Around

A	S	O	R	X	R	E	T	D	B	R	A	N	T
S	T	A	L	L	E	M	M	W	D	A	I	R	E
B	I	T	Z	A	I	O	O	A	A	I	O	G	K
L	R	S	C	T	N	L	N	L	D	T	J	A	N
A	R	J	A	S	S	A	D	K	A	O	I	L	A
N	U	O	N	J	B	R	U	S	H	S	M	L	L
K	P	H	T	O	R	M	R	O	S	A	S	O	B
E	S	N	E	E	I	B	O	K	A	D	L	E	E
G	K	E	R	O	D	J	R	C	E	D	O	T	S
R	S	A	D	D	L	E	B	A	Y	A	H	N	T
A	H	A	R	N	E	S	S	T	D	R	T	O	R
I	O	B	O	F	R	D	Y	R	X	V	R	M	A
N	E	R	A	G	A	L	L	O	P	T	I	U	W
R	S	E	S	K	A	L	O	M	M	J	G	M	C

Page 75

Horse Sense

1. 14, 13, 23,
2. 8
3. Tuesday is the horse.
4. 4
5. 8 + 1 - 3 = 6

   5 + 2 + 2 - 3 = 6

   3 + 7 - 4 - 2 = 4

   9 - 1 + 7 - 7 = 8

   or

   9 - 1 - 7 + 7 = 8

Page 78

Poodle Parlor

4	1	6
5	2	3

Page 80

Houdini's Great Escape!

Page 80 (cont.)

Paw-sible Solutions

Page 81

Water World

angel fish	hammerhead shark
blue whale	jellyfish
box turtle	lionfish
electric eel	seahorse
fiddler crab	swordfish
goldfish	tiger shark

Pages 82-83

Walk on the Wild Side

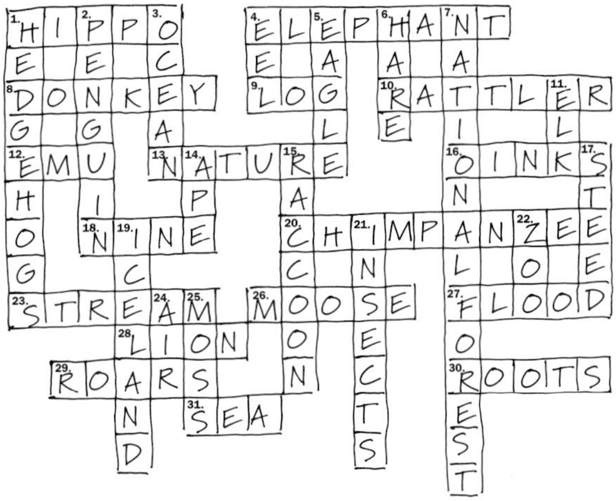

Page 84

Leap, Frog!

1st: Peeper

2nd: Croakie

3rd: Ribbit

4th: Bull

Page 85

Pet Patrol

R	O	M	D	A	L	M	A	T	I	A	N	O	T
A	S	A	A	F	T	O	S	I	A	M	E	S	E
H	L	N	C	I	F	I	G	H	L	U	R	H	R
A	E	X	H	S	N	P	B	B	A	T	A	O	R
M	A	I	S	H	O	E	I	B	F	T	B	R	I
S	B	E	H	J	B	R	C	P	A	E	Y	T	E
T	G	I	U	O	D	S	D	O	B	R	S	H	R
E	I	L	N	E	R	I	X	N	O	O	S	A	E
R	P	L	D	B	E	A	G	L	E	N	I	I	S
C	A	O	S	I	A	N	E	S	U	E	N	R	E
O	E	C	T	O	R	R	A	P	O	B	I	E	G
L	N	R	E	T	R	I	E	V	E	R	A	S	N
L	I	E	L	A	B	A	P	E	R	S	N	R	I
Y	U	X	M	B	X	O	D	A	L	M	A	O	K
M	G	O	A	B	N	T	E	R	R	E	F	H	E
A	N	B	H	Y	H	O	R	E	L	D	O	O	P

Pages 86-87

Kitty City

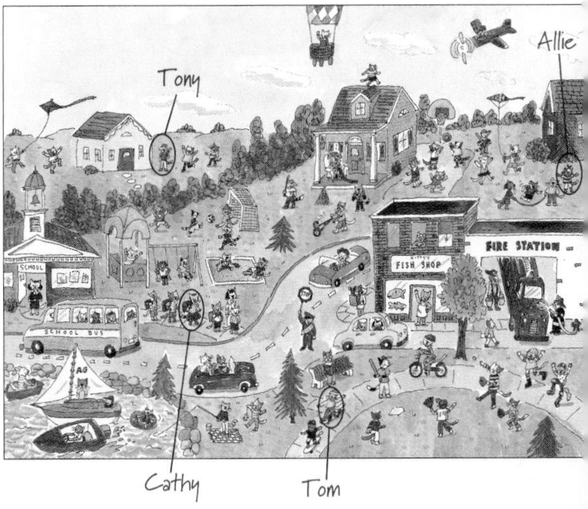

Place
Stamp
Here

American Girl®

PO BOX 620497
MIDDLETON WI 53562-0497

BUSINESS REPLY MAIL

FIRST-CLASS MAIL PERMIT NO. 190 BOONE IA

POSTAGE WILL BE PAID BY ADDRESSEE

NO POSTAGE
NECESSARY
IF MAILED
IN THE
UNITED STATES

AmericanGirl®

PO BOX 37311
BOONE IA 50037-2311